Life's Journeys
According to
Mister Rogers

ALSO BY

FRED ROGERS

The World According to Mister Rogers

Life's Journeys According to Mister Rogers

THINGS TO REMEMBER ALONG THE WAY

FRED ROGERS

HYPERION

NEW YORK

Copyright © 2005 Family Communications,
Inc.

Library of Congress Cataloging-in-Publication
Data
Rogers, Fred.
   Life's journeys according to Mister Rogers:
   things to remember along the way/Fred
   Rogers.
      p. cm.
   ISBN 1-4013-0169-X
   1. Conduct of life. 2. Self-acceptance. I. Title.

BJ1581.2.R633 2005
170'.44—dc22   2004059774

Hyperion books are available for special
promotions and premiums. For details
contact Michael Rentas, Assistant Director,
Inventory Operations, Hyperion, 77 West 66th
Street, 11th floor, New York, New York 10023,
or call 212-456-0133.

FIRST EDITION

10 9 8 7 6 5 4 3 2 1

This book is dedicated
to all our neighbors
on their journeys,
and to all who
have been with us on ours.

CONTENTS

Life's Journeys
According to
Mister Rogers

FOREWORD
by Joanne Rogers

When the day turns into night,
And you're way beyond my sight,
I think of you.

One of my treasures is a photo of a sunset that Fred sent to me, with those words from one of his songs on a little note that he put on the back. Fred had taken that photo when he was in Nantucket without me for a bit. He loved being on the other side of the camera—taking pictures! That photo and those few words have carried me through a lot these days. In fact, I've put the photo in a frame, and I set that note in a corner, right in front. Even though he's "way beyond my sight," I'm still being nourished by his words. It's such a comfort to know that others are, too.

Life is a curious journey. Certainly when Fred and I married, neither he nor I expected to find ourselves on the road that was ahead of us. I'd have to say, though, that from his senior year of college on, Fred knew what kind of journey he wanted. Early on, he was convinced that television could be an inspiring and positive force, especially for children, and he felt a calling to be a part of that mission.

It still took him a long time to get where he wanted to be. Along the way, he used his time and his energies to gather what he felt might strengthen him for that calling. Somehow, from what he saw on television in the early 1950s, he knew in his heart that there could be a connection between television, the real needs of human beings (particularly children), and spirituality. All through his life, he focused on learning all he could about each of those three elements—and that's why he was able to weave them so skillfully together in the magnificent tapestry of his lifework.

Even when the world around him was changing, becoming fast-paced and materialistic, even hectic and violent at times, even when he seemed to be going against the current and some were urging him to pick up the pace of his program, Fred was determined to stay the course. Anyone who was close to him knew about his "steel backbone." A lot of people might be surprised to think of him that way, but he was strong-willed and determined. The mentors he trusted most supported his decision to continue on what he knew was the right path—to be himself!

My involvement in Fred's work was primarily as a fan and as background support. I did lots of cheering—from the sidelines! I came into our marriage with a master's degree in piano performance. So it was natural for me as a young wife to become busy in the music community of Pittsburgh, teaching piano and playing concerts.

After our first child was born, I put the piano on the back burner for a few years. But as the boys grew older, I went back to it and got together again with my college friend and duo-piano partner, Jeannine Morrison, for concerts. I thought it was important to continue using what talent I have. To be perfectly honest, I started playing again because it was fun and because I knew it was good for me. Just as exercise keeps our bodies fit (if we do it! hmmmm), so I truly believe the piano work keeps my brain agile.

I also had an ulterior motive: the hope that my sons would eventually feel freer, knowing that I wasn't solely invested in them and their lives. As an only child, I knew the ambivalence of being the subject of my parents' near-adoration. Part of me thoroughly enjoyed their attention, and at the same time I felt a definite burden of trying to please both of them—a difficult journey at times, to be sure.

Fred and I always allowed each other our own space. Fred's sister wasn't adopted into the family until he was eleven. So essentially, we were both only children, and it was obvious to both of us that we each needed our own space. But even when we were apart, we were connected.

I couldn't help getting caught up in Fred's world. For the last twenty-five years of his life, everywhere we went, people would come up to him to say hello. He loved hearing their stories. One of the worst jobs was moving him along in a crowd! Everyone wanted to talk with him. And he loved their stories. He would just keep on asking questions so he could get to know more about them. He had a heart that had room for everyone, and he was fascinated by other people's journeys.

That's probably why he loved the fan mail so much. He always brought home copies of letters to share with me. In his answers, he wanted to give the same attention and respect that he felt the writers had put into their letters. There was even a time in the mid-1960s when he'd bring the mail home and after the boys were in bed, we would sit at the dining room table while he'd write out the answers. It's a good thing we weren't paid by the hour because it was mighty slow work. We'd have to stop and read almost every one out loud to each other!

Fred is still with me most of the time. There is hardly a minute that I don't think about him. A lot of my language contains "we" and "our"—he's so much a part of my ongoing journey. I am still getting letters from people who continue to care about his work. Their stories are real treasures and warm my heart. I have the boxes of mail in the corner of my dining room—most of them answered and some yet to do. You know, he wasn't a "TV star" to them. They tell me that they thought of him as a personal friend and that he meant so much to their children. That would've pleased him so much! Almost all of them added something like "and we watch, too." It touches me deeply that these loving "neighbors" want to share their sense of Fred with me.

After Fred died, I was asked to take his place at a number of events where he'd been scheduled to give a speech. Fred had always spoken so beautifully, and I really wasn't comfortable taking his place. But when I realized that these audiences were Fred's loving friends and that they didn't expect me to be Fred, I actually started to enjoy it! Now I speak occasionally, and I just try to be myself.

Another big part of my life now is my involvement with

those who are committed to carrying on Fred's legacy, especially the amazingly gifted staff members at Family Communications, Inc., who have become my extended family. (FCI is the nonprofit company that Fred founded in 1971.) Much of Fred's spirit is still there at FCI, where so many hours of his life were spent. Some of my favorite times are my visits there at their offices. It's a great comfort to know that this FCI family, who is so knowledgeable about Fred's philosophy in working with children and families, is as invested in his legacy as I am.

On the horizon is The Fred M. Rogers Center for Early Learning and Children's Media. It's still in the planning stages at St. Vincent College in Fred's hometown of Latrobe, PA. Fred had been in on the early discussions for it, and I've been fascinated to be involved with so many of his friends and colleagues in forging a path for it.

Probably the best part of my work now is that I've met some wonderful people. And I've gotten to know them. We've kept in touch, calling now and then, exchanging e-mails, visiting when they're in town, sharing memories, jokes, and funny stories (I do love to laugh!).

Wouldn't it be nice if we could just tell ourselves, "Okay, you've grieved. Your time to grieve is up. Now it's time to get your act together." But it's not like that for me. Some days I feel energized. Some days I feel depleted. Grieving can be exhausting! Since I was a child, I've had an irrational fear that if I start crying, I'll not be able to stop. The tears do come sometimes when I'm alone and missing Fred—sometimes tears of anger that he was taken from us too soon. But then I try to remember my overriding feeling at the time he went to heaven—that feeling of blessed relief that his pain and suffering were over.

After Fred died, I didn't even have the energy or inclination to play the piano. For nine whole months I didn't touch the keyboard. What brought me back was that Jeannine and I had a concert commitment. Journeys can be like that—when we're at an "in-between" time, something often happens to push us on toward taking a step or starting a new direction. So I finally started working at the piano again, and thankfully my fingers remembered the feel of the piano keys!

One of Fred's favorite writers was the theologian Henri Nouwen. He had read almost all of his writings, and they became good friends. Through their long phone conversations, Fred was aware of the importance to Henri of "dying well." That's how Henri handled the end of his life a few years ago. It was what Fred wanted in his own life, too—to die well. I've often thought how proud Henri would be of the way Fred handled the end of his journey. He did it honestly, not denying it. When he told his long-term staff at FCI that he had been diagnosed with stomach cancer and was about to have surgery, he said, "Here we are on another journey." At the end, it was his beloved heaven that gave him hope.

One of our friends asked Fred about his thoughts on heaven when she was taking a walk with him on a Nantucket beach a few years ago. I'll bet there was a twinkle in his eye when he told her, "Oh, I think there will be a lot of people surprised to see who's there!" Fred would never want anyone to think they might not be worthy of getting through heaven's gate. His God loved everyone—just the way they were! And we loved him, too—just the way he was.

Who You Are
Right Now

There are many times that I wish I had heard that "just who you are at this moment, with the way that you're feeling, is fine. You don't have to be anything more than who you are right now." I'd like to think it's also something that's happened to me through the years, that I'm more able to accept myself as I happen to be, rather than as somebody thought I should be.

Each person in the world is a unique human being, and each has unique human potential. One of the important tasks of growing is the *discovery* of this uniqueness: the discovery of "who I am" in each of us— of "who I am" in relation to all those whom I meet.

Anything that's human is mentionable, and anything that is mentionable can be more manageable. When we can talk about our feelings, they become less overwhelming, less upsetting, and less scary. The people we trust with that important talk can help us know that we're not alone.

We can't be expected to leave the unhappy and angry parts of ourselves at the door before coming in. We all need to feel that we can bring the whole of ourselves to the people who care about us.

I believe that at the center of the universe there dwells a loving spirit who longs for all that's best in all of creation, a spirit who knows the great potential of each planet as well as each person, and little by little will love us into being more than we ever dreamed possible. That loving spirit would rather die than give up on any one of us.

When I was a kid, I was shy and overweight. I was a perfect target for ridicule.

One day (how well I remember that day, and it's more than sixty years ago!) we got out of school early, and I started to walk home by myself. It wasn't long before I sensed I was being followed—by a whole group of boys. As I walked faster, I looked around, and they started to call my name and came closer and closer and got louder and louder.

"Freddy, hey, fat Freddy. We're going to get you, Freddy."

I resented those kids for not seeing beyond my fatness or my shyness. And I didn't know that it was all right to resent it, to feel bad about it, even to feel very sad about it. I didn't know it was all right to feel any of those things, because the advice I got from the grown-ups was, "Just let on you don't care, then nobody will bother you."

What I actually did was mourn. I cried to myself whenever I was alone. I cried through my fingers as I made up songs on the piano. I sought out stories of other people who were poor in spirit, and I felt for them.

I started to look behind the things that people did and said; and little by little, concluded that Saint-Exupéry was absolutely right when he wrote in *The Little Prince*:

"What is essential is invisible to the eyes." So after a lot of sadness, I began a lifelong search for what is essential, what it is about my neighbor that doesn't meet the eye.

"Let on you don't care, then nobody will bother you." Those who gave me that advice were well-meaning people; but, of course, I *did* care, and somehow along the way I caught the belief that God cares, too; that the divine presence cares for those of us who are hurting and that presence is everywhere. I don't know exactly how this came to me, maybe through one of my teachers or the town librarian, maybe through a musician or a minister—definitely across some holy ground. And, of course, it could have come from the grandfather I was named for: Fred McFeely, who used to say to me after we'd had a visit together, "Freddy, you made this day a special day for me."

My hunch is that the beginning of my belief in the caring nature of God came from *all* of those people—all of those extraordinary, ordinary people who believed that I was more than I thought I was—all those saints who helped a fat, shy kid to see more clearly what was really essential.

I realize that it isn't very fashionable
to talk about some things as being holy;
nevertheless, if we ever want to rid
ourselves of personal and corporate
emptiness, brokenness, loneliness, and
fear, we will have to allow ourselves room
for that which we cannot see, hear,
touch, or control.

If we're really honest with ourselves, there are probably times when we think, "What possible use can I be in this world? What need is there for somebody like me to fill?" That's one of the deeper mysteries. Then God's grace comes to us in the form of another person who tells us we have been of help, and what a blessing that is.

The greatest loss that we all have to deal with is the loss of the image of ourselves as a perfect person.

If I'm sad about something, and I dismiss my sadness by saying, "Oh, well, it was for the best," then I'm probably not willing or able to explore how I'm feeling. If I'm angry with someone, and I say, "Oh, it doesn't matter, I don't care," then I probably don't know what I'm really feeling.

On the other hand, if we can allow ourselves to be gentle with ourselves no matter what our feelings may be, we have the chance of discovering the very deep roots of who we are.

My personal introduction to the Dalai Lama was by way of television—in a hotel room. I was in Washington, D.C., preparing for a conference on children and the media and was looking for a certain news program when I happened upon His Holiness saying, "Someone else's action should not determine your response." I was so intrigued, I wrote down those words, turned off the television, and thought about nothing else the whole evening.

"Someone else's action should not determine your response." It sounds so simple, doesn't it? And yet what if someone else's action should be shouting angry words at us or hitting us with a rotten tomato? That doesn't affect what we do in response? Not if our compassion is genuine. Not if our love is the kind the Dalai Lama advocates.

FROM THE SONG

I'm Still Myself Inside

I can put on a hat, or put on a coat,
Or wear a pair of glasses or sail in a boat.
I can change all my names
  and find a place to hide.
I can do almost anything,
  but I'm still myself inside.

I can go far away, or dream anything,
Or wear a scary costume or act like a king.
I can change all my names
  and find a place to hide.
I can do almost anything, but I'm still
  myself,
I'm still myself,
I'm still myself inside.

You are a very special person. There is only
one like you in the whole world. There's
never been anyone exactly like you before,
and there never will be again. Only you.
And people can like you exactly as you are.

Yo-Yo Ma is one of the most other-oriented geniuses I've ever known. His music comes from a place very deep within his being. During a master class, Yo-Yo gently led young cellists into understandings about their instruments, their music, and their "selves" which, some of them told me later, they would carry with them forever.

I can still see the face of one young man who had just finished playing a movement of a Brahms cello sonata when Yo-Yo said, "Nobody else can make the sound you make." Of course, he meant it as a compliment to the young man; nevertheless, he meant that also for everyone in the class. Nobody else can make the sound you make. Nobody can choose to make that particular sound in that particular way.

Nobody else can live the life you live. And even though no human being is perfect, we always have the chance to bring what's unique about us to life.

We all have different gifts, so we all have different ways of saying to the world who we are.

What's been important in my understanding of myself and others is the fact that each one of us is so much more than any one thing. A sick child is much more than his or her sickness. A person with a disability is much, much more than a handicap. A pediatrician is more than a medical doctor. You're *much* more than your job description or your age or your income or your output.

One of my mentors, Dr. C., worked with us every week for thirty years. He listened to ideas for scripts and songs and toys and books and records and speeches; and, over that time, he helped all of us who consulted with him realize that somehow we were uniquely suited for what we were doing.

Through those years, each one of us in our particular neighborhood grew at our own pace along the road of maturity both professionally and personally. Dr. C. had that innate gift in everything that he said and did which allowed people who worked with him to develop from within.

As I think back on those thirty years of work with Dr. C., I realize anew that he never hurried us. We were never made to feel that we had to be somebody that we were not, yet we were always encouraged to choose to be the best of who we were at the moment. Indeed, our development was far from overnight—we become who we are over time.

There's a part of all of us that longs to know that even what's weakest about us is still redeemable and can ultimately count for something good.

Shyness isn't something that just children feel. Anybody can feel shy. And one reason we feel that way is that we're not sure people will like us just the way we are.

One of my seminary professors, Dr. Orr, often talked with great poignancy about Henry, a student who had come to the seminary with a degree in classic literature and a fine working knowledge of Greek and Latin as well as several modern languages. He remembered this young man as being brilliant and yet always receiving with such grace the offers of others. "He never put on airs," Dr. Orr said. "You always felt he really respected everybody else."

It seems that this young man was a perfectionist. For him every word had to be just so. It was excruciating for him to give a sermon unless he felt it was letter-perfect; consequently, it took him two months to write one sermon. Even though he tried hard, it became clear to him that he was not going to be suited for the parish ministry. Eventually, he dropped out of seminary and took a job at a local department store.

Dr. Orr didn't hear from him for a long while, so one day, he stopped in the store to see how Henry was faring. It happened to be Henry's day off, but his coworkers talked with Dr. Orr about him. The more they talked, the more Dr. Orr realized that the people at the store knew nothing about this fellow employee's extensive education. What they did know was what had happened in their department after his arrival. "This department was filled with all kinds of jealousy and pettiness. It was a miserable place to work before Henry came," a person told Dr. Orr. "But after he had been here awhile, somehow all of that miserable stuff seemed to disappear. We all got working together, and well, it's different with him here. He is like a minister in more ways than anyone ever knows. You say you know Henry? Well, you are blessed, too, then."

Dr. Orr finally contacted Henry, and the two of them read Greek literature together for ten years before Henry died. When Dr. Orr talked about him, he would invariably say, "To think there were people at the seminary—and elsewhere—who called it a waste for Henry to have done what he did, working at that department store." Then Dr. Orr would add, "Henry probably had one of the greatest ministries I know. I feel privileged to have been his friend."

When people help us to feel good about who
we are, they are really helping us to love
the meaning of what we create in this life.
It seems to me that the most essential
element in the development of any creation
must be love—a love that begins in the
simple expressions of care for a little child,
and, once received, goes on to mature
into responsible feelings about ourselves
and others.

I wonder if we might pledge ourselves to remember what life is really all about—not to be afraid that we're less flashy than the next, not to worry that our influence is not that of a tornado, but rather that of a grain of sand in an oyster! Do we have that kind of patience?

It's really easy to fall into the trap of believing that what we *do* is more important than what we *are*. Of course, it's the opposite that's true: What we *are* ultimately determines what we *do*!

I need thinking time when someone asks me a searching question. I wonder why it seems to be so uncomfortable for many people to wait through the silence. People of all ages have deep feelings, and if we have the patience to wait through the silence, it's often astounding what people will tell us.

Here's a gift you may not have expected. It's a gift for you to give yourself. Sometime in your day today, try to turn off all the noises you can around you, and give yourself some "quiet time." In the silence, let yourself think about something. Or if possible . . . think about nothing.

Most of us have so few moments like that in our lives. There's noise everywhere. There are some places we can't even escape it. Television and radio are probably the worst culprits. They are very seductive. It's so tempting for some people to turn on the television set or the radio when they first walk into a room or get in the car . . . to fill any space with noise. I wonder what some people are afraid might happen in the silence. Some of us must have forgotten how nourishing silence can be.

That kind of solitude goes by many names. It may be called "meditation" or "deep relaxation," "quiet time" or "downtime." In some circles, it may even be criticized as "daydreaming." Whatever it's called, it's a time away from outside stimulation, during which inner turbulence can settle, and we have a chance to become more familiar with ourselves.

How many times have you noticed it's the little quiet moments in the midst of life that seem to give the rest extra-special meaning?

I can see how all the interests I had as I was growing up served me well in the work I finally chose to do—writing songs, making puppets talk, thinking up stories, looking for helpers. It's very important, no matter what you may do professionally, to keep alive some of the healthy interests of your youth. Children's play is not just kids' stuff. Children's play is rather the stuff of most future inventions. Think how many people played about going to the moon before that was ever a reality. Let your imagination help you to know the truth about your identity.

Our biological makeup at birth has much to do with who we become, but so do our environment and our psychological development from one stage to another. And how we grow with all our unique endowments will influence how people will respond to us.

Who we are in the present includes who we were in the past.

Letting go is seldom easy—whether it's letting go of our children, our parents, or our childhood feelings. But just as the root systems of plants often have to be divided for healthy growth to continue, the different generations within a family may have to pull apart for a while for each to find its own healthy identity.

Being creative is part of being human.
Everyone is creative. Each person's
creativity finds different form, that's true;
but without creativity of some kind, I
doubt that we'd get through many of the
problems that life poses.

One of our chief jobs in life, it seems
to me, is to realize how rare and valuable
each one of us really is—that each of us has
something which no one else has—or ever
will have—something inside which is
unique to all time.

Years ago, a friend gave me a piece of calligraphy which I have always kept in my office. It's a quotation from *The Little Prince* by Antoine de Saint-Exupéry that reads, *"L'essentiel est invisible pour les yeux."* What is essential is invisible to the eyes.

What is essential about *you* that is invisible to the eye? What are some of the things about your very being that allow you to look to the years ahead with confidence?

"The outside is never as much as the inside. . . ." As you may know by now, that's one of the major themes of our work: The invisible essential. Oh, the outsides of life are important, but the insides are what enhance so much of the rest.

When I graduated from college, I had little notion of how I'd ever be able to put together all the interests that I had. It took a good deal of time, and my parents probably wondered if I'd ever be able to make anything of myself.

But I'll never forget the sense of wholeness I felt when I finally realized, after a lot of help from a lot of people, what, in fact, I really was. I was not just a songwriter or a language buff or a student of human development or a telecommunicator, but someone who could use every talent that had ever been given to me in the service of children (and their families).

I can tell you that it was that particular focus that made all the difference for me. I can also tell you that the directions weren't written on the back of my college diploma. They came ever so slowly for me; and ever so firmly, I trusted that they would emerge.

All I can say is, it's worth the struggle to discover who you really are and how you, in your own way, can put life together as something that means a lot to you. It's a miracle when you finally discover whom you're best equipped to serve—and we're all equipped to serve in some way.

Are you able to believe in a loving presence who desires the best for you and the whole universe?

With all the sadness and destruction, negativity and rage expressed throughout the world, it's tough not to wonder where the loving presence is. Well, we don't have to look very far. Deep within each of us is a spark of the divine just waiting to be used to light up a dark place. The only thing is—we have the free choice of using it or not. That's part of the mysterious truth of who we human beings are.

What are some of the ways of showing and telling who you are and how you're feeling? They may be sports or homemaking or art or music or crafts or science or math or dance or selling or public speaking. Whatever they may be, and if you know they're healthy, try to keep embracing them, love them, give them room to grow inside yourself, because those gifts of expression are so unique to you.

Loving
and
Being
Loved

I wonder what memories of yours will persist as you go on in life. My hunch is that the most important will have to do with feelings of loving and being loved—family, friends, teachers, shopkeepers—whoever's been close to you. As you continue to grow, you'll find many ways of expressing your love and you'll discover more and more ways in which others express their love for you.

It's a mistake to think that we have to
be lovely to be loved by human beings
or by God.

Anyone who has ever been able to sustain good work has had at least one person—and often many—who have believed in him or her. We just don't get to be competent human beings without a lot of different investments from others.

For a long time, I've wondered why I felt like bowing when people showed their appreciation for the work that I've been privileged to do. It's been a kind of natural response to a feeling of great gratitude. What I've come to understand is that we who bow are probably—whether we know it or not—acknowledging the presence of the sacred. We're bowing to the sacred in our neighbor.

You see, I believe that appreciation is a holy thing—that when we look for what's best in a person we happen to be with at the moment, we're doing what God does all the time. So in loving and appreciating our neighbor, we're participating in something sacred.

As I bow, I always feel like saying, "Thank you, thank you, thank you."

As a relationship matures, you start to see that just being there for each other is the most important thing you can do, just being there to listen and be sorry with them, to be happy with them, to share all that there is to share.

The best gifts are often wrapped in the most unspectacular ways.

You've probably had many fancy wrapped-up gifts—gifts which dazzle the eyes and impress the neighbors; nevertheless, isn't it the "heartsurprise" that lingers in your memory and serves to nourish you from year to year?

When the Day Turns into Night

When the day turns into night,
And you're way beyond my sight,
I think of you, I think of you.

When the night turns into day,
And you still are far away,
I think of you, I think of you.

Even when I am not here,
We still can be so very near.
I want you to know, my dear,
I think of you.

There isn't any one of us who hasn't felt the loss of someone who's "way beyond our sight." From childhood on, we human beings know the pain of separation as well as the joy of reunion. There is something so comforting to realize that life goes on one way or another—even when those we love are way beyond our sight.

There was a story going around about the Special Olympics. For the hundred-yard dash, there were nine contestants, all of them so-called physically or mentally disabled. All nine of them assembled at the starting line and, at the sound of the gun, they took off. But one little boy didn't get very far. He stumbled and fell and hurt his knee and began to cry.

The other eight children heard the boy crying. They slowed down, turned around, and ran back to him—every one of them ran back to him. The little boy got up, and he and the rest of the runners linked their arms together and joyfully walked to the finish line.

They all finished the race at the same time. And when they did, everyone in the stadium stood up and clapped and whistled and cheered for a long, long time. And you know why? Because deep down we know that what matters in this life is more than winning for ourselves. What really matters is helping others win, too, even if it means slowing down and changing our course now and then.

Our world hangs like a magnificent jewel in the vastness of space. Every one of us is a part of this jewel; and, in the perspective of infinity, our differences are infinitesimal. We are intimately related. May we never even pretend that we are not.

Finding out that we are one of a kind could be a lonely and frightening thing without the reassurance of knowing that we belong to humankind, and that all humans laugh and cry about many of the same things; that all have similar hopes and fears; that all have many of the same needs; and that those needs are best met by other human beings who can love us for both our similarities and our differences.

Every human being has value. This is the basis of all healthy relationships. Through living each day as it is given to me, I've learned that. It cannot be "taught," but it can be "caught" from those who live their lives right along with us. What a privilege to be able to look for the good in our neighbor!

The roots of all our lives go very, very deep, and we can't really understand a person unless we have the chance of knowing who that person has been, and what that person has done and liked and suffered and believed.

How our words are understood doesn't depend just on how we express our ideas. It also depends on how someone receives what we're saying. I think the most important part about communicating is the listening we do beforehand. When we can truly respect what someone brings to what we're offering, it makes the communication all the more meaningful.

We speak with more than our mouths. We listen with more than our ears.

I remember one of my seminary professors saying people who were able to appreciate others—who looked for what was good and healthy and kind—were about as close as you could get to God—to the eternal good. And those people who were always looking for what was *bad* about themselves and others were really on the side of evil. "That's what evil wants," he would say. "Evil wants us to feel so terrible about who we are and who we know, that we'll look with condemning eyes on anybody who happens to be with us at the moment." I encourage you to look for the good where you are and embrace it.

More than 1,500 years ago, the Roman philosopher Boethius wrote this sentence: "Oh happy race of mortals if your hearts are ruled, as is the universe, by love."

I know how important it is to give up our expectations of perfection in any arena of our lives. I know I've tried hard; and yet, every once in a while, I'll entertain the old longing: "Maybe if I could make at least one perfect *segment* of a program . . . ," and I find myself in the trap again.

That doesn't mean we can't produce some highly satisfying moments both for ourselves and others, but it's important to give up—maybe daily—the longing to be perfect. Of course, I think we want it so strongly because we reason that if we are perfect (if we do a perfect job), we will be perfectly lovable. What a heavy burden! Thank God we don't have to *earn* every bit of love that comes our way.

A friend of mine visited a beautiful monastery where a dozen monks—most of them in their 70s and 80s—were living. This is a place which once had a population of sixty active men studying and following a very strict rule of living: praying together seven different times a day, seven days a week. They worked hard, and they were successful.

My friend asked one of the monks why he felt that over the years the community had dwindled from sixty to twelve. And his reply was: "We did everything right, but somewhere in all that living and praying and successful working, we lost the most important thing of all, the thing that was so contagious and attracted people to us: We lost the naked love. Little by little the success replaced the love."

The old monk ended by saying, "Oh, sure, you can have love *and* success, but the love has to remain first—always first: natural, accepting, affirming, inclusive, naked love."

Love and success, always in that order. It's that simple *and* that difficult.

Feeling good about ourselves is essential in our being able to love others.

Relationships are like dances in which people try to find whatever happens to be the mutual rhythm in their lives.

Caring comes from the Gothic word *kara*, which means "to lament." So caring is not what a powerful person gives to a weaker one. Caring is a matter of being there . . . lamenting right along with the one who laments.

A person can grow to his or her fullest capacity only in mutually caring relationships with others.

I think it's so great that people can be in a relationship with each other for the now and not bring a whole lot of baggage from their past and a whole lot of anxiety about the future to the present moment.

All we're ever asked to do in this life is to treat our neighbor—especially our neighbor who is in need—exactly as we would hope to be treated ourselves. That's our ultimate responsibility.

The older I get, the more I come to understand that the things we possess can never bring us ultimate happiness. Contrary to what's implied in commercials, nothing we buy can ever take away our loneliness or fill our emptiness or heal our brokenness. You know yourself—way down deep—that what really matters is how we live this life with our neighbors (those who we happen to be with at the moment). That's what really matters. That's really *all* that matters.

There is a close relationship between truth
and trust.

Where would any of us be without teachers—
without people who have passion for their
art or their science or their craft and love it
right in front of us? What would any of us
do without teachers passing on to us what
they know is essential about life?

There are three ways to ultimate success:

The first way is to be kind.

The second way is to be kind.

The third way is to be kind.

I don't think anyone can grow unless he's loved exactly as he is now, appreciated for what he is rather than what he will be.

The receiving in life to me is one of the greatest gifts that we give another person. And it's very hard. Because when you give, you're in much greater control. But when you receive something—you're vulnerable.

Honesty is often very hard. The truth is often painful. But the freedom it can bring is worth the trying.

The toughest thing is to love somebody who has done something mean to you—especially when that somebody is yourself. Look inside yourself and find that loving part of you. Take good care of that part because it helps you love your neighbor.

The outside things of life certainly do change and often quickly, but the inside things remain. Our parents and their parents and their parents—all of us—were created by Love. Love with a capital L. And we spend our lives trying to recognize that we truly *are* lovable and capable of loving.

We're all on a journey—each one of us.
And if we can be sensitive to the person
who happens to be our "neighbor", that, to
me, is the greatest challenge as well as the
greatest pleasure. Because if you're trusted,
then people will allow you to share their
inner garden—what greater gift!

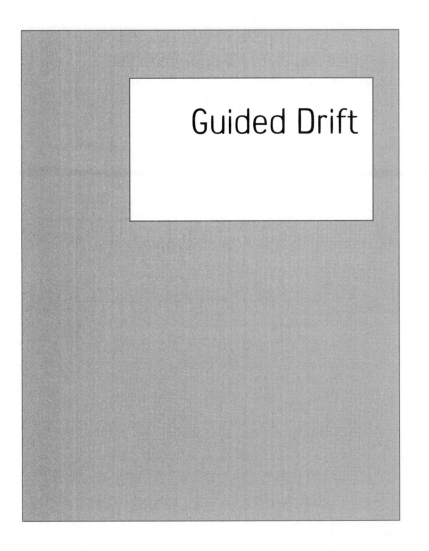

Guided Drift

I am glad that I've been able to do what I've done and not been sidetracked along the way. A teacher of mine calls it guided drift. Isn't that wonderful? You're drifting, and yet you've got a rudder.

I saw a friend who's a freelance writer and asked him what he was working on. "Nothing right now," he answered. "You know how it is for freelancers. But at times like this I tell myself I'm 'between opportunities.' That way I don't have to feel I'm nowhere."

There's often a tendency for us to hurry through transitions. We may feel that these transitions are "nowhere at all" compared to what's gone before or what we anticipate is next to come. But you are somewhere . . . you're "between."

Sometimes it surprises me to think that my work on that first children's program was almost by chance! Isn't it mysterious how so many wonderful things in life come to us seemingly without our planning? We start traveling down one street, and we find ourselves interested in something we never expected on a side street; and as we explore it, the side street becomes the main road for us.

Transitions are almost always signs of growth, but they can bring feelings of loss. To get somewhere new, we may have to leave somewhere else behind.

We'd all like to feel self-reliant and capable of coping with whatever adversity comes our way, but that's not how most human beings are made. It's my belief that the capacity to accept help is inseparable from the capacity to give help when our turn comes to be strong.

It can sometimes be difficult to ask for support when we need it, but having someone we can count on to stick with us through the tough times can make those times much more bearable.

A friend of mine was in a taxi in Washington, D.C., going slowly past the National Archives, when he noticed the words on the cornerstone of the building: "The past is prologue." He read them out loud to the taxi driver and said, "What do you think that means, 'The past is prologue'?"

The taxi driver said, "I think it means, 'Man, you ain't seen nothin' yet!'"

I recently learned that in an average lifetime a person walks about sixty-five thousand miles. That's two and a half times around the world. I wonder where your steps will take you. I wonder how you'll use the rest of the miles you're given.

Have you ever worked as hard as you knew how and people still didn't appreciate you? What do you do? You either give up or you keep on.

What will you do about your hard times? I wonder what is in store for you and what you will make of it. What kind of opportunities will you have to use the talents you've been given? Who will help you? How will you respond to your successes? How will you help the children in your life to grow and develop into confident, helpful adults? How will you respond to people with obvious disabilities? Will you use your own disability (we all have them, you know) to understand or to separate you from your neighbor? What kind of person are you going to be?

Sometimes it takes years and years of experimentation to realize who we can be . . . what we can make of what has come to us. No one would have ever predicted that Mahatma Gandhi would become the person to dramatically change the life of people in India. He even went to England when he was young to explore whether it might be better to be an Englishman. But look how he put it all together later on.

Maybe it's happened to you already when you can actually integrate what you've learned with your own personality—

when you can actually use your education to be who you want to be, to choose out of that mixed bag of explorations what you want to call yourself. That's when your education adds an extra measure of excitement!

There are all kinds of artists in the world. If people can combine the talent that they have inside of them with the hard work that it takes to develop it, they can become true artists.

As work grows out of play, an attitude toward work grows with it—an attitude that may persist through our workaday life. That attitude can have a lot to do with how we accept challenges, how we cope with failures, and whether we can find in the jobs we do, the inner fulfillment that makes working worthwhile, in and of itself.

In 1963, President John F. Kennedy went to Dallas, Texas. He was going to speak there. If he had lived, these are some of the words that he had written to say: "We ask that we may be worthy of our power and responsibility—that we may *exercise* our strength with wisdom." It's hard work to *exercise* our strength with wisdom, to be responsible stewards of what we've been given. You know how hard it is. You can't satisfy all the desires of those who ask, but you can translate some of the care you have inside of yourself to action on the outside.

Teilhard de Chardin, a 19th century philosopher, writes that someone scrawled the following words on the bulletin board of the great Notre-Dame Cathedral:
"*Le monde demain appartiendra à ceux qui lui ont apporté la plus grande espérance.*"
The world tomorrow will belong to those who brought it the greatest hope.

There is much more to independence than
learning to master new skills. One of the
most important parts of independence is
learning to form new relationships with
other people.

I feel I've been greatly blessed by many people I've been able to meet and come to know. Sure, I've worked hard. You don't choose a job and expect not to work hard. But you can expect that you don't have to do it alone. Nobody should have to do it alone.

There are times when explanations, no matter how reasonable, just don't seem to help.

It may be that the most important mastery we achieve early on is not the mastery of a particular skill or particular piece of knowledge, but rather the mastery of the patience and persistence that learning requires, along with the ability to expect and accept mistakes and the feelings of disappointment they may bring.

I enjoy working on our program, but, of course, as with any kind of work, we have some frustrating times. Often those are when we have problems with the equipment when we're taping in the studio. It can also be frustrating when I am trying to write something and can't seem to get an idea that feels right. Sometimes, when I'm working on a script or composing a song, writing flows easily, but there are lots of times it doesn't. It's probably true that all writers have frustrating and discouraging moments.

Sometimes it helps me to get away from the work—by taking a walk, sitting in a quiet

room, listening to music, talking with a
friend. Sometimes I just go over to the piano
and play out my feelings through music.
That kind of break seems to nourish me, and
I can come back renewed.

When we study how our ancestors dealt with challenges, we can (hopefully) learn from their successes *and* failures.

Someone once asked Edison if he was disappointed after trying 382 ways of making a lightbulb. He answered that he wasn't. He was glad that he now knew 382 ways *not* to try.

The media shows the tiniest percentage of what people do. There are millions and millions of people doing wonderful things all over the world, and they're generally not the ones being touted in the news.

Please Don't Think It's Funny

In the long, long trip of growing,
There are stops along the way
For thoughts of all the soft things
And a look at yesterday.
For a chance to fill our feelings
With comfort and with ease,
And then tell the new tomorrow:
"You can come now when you please."

We don't have to think it's funny when we feel like we need some extra comfort. I sometimes sing about that to children, but, as you know, I believe there's a child somewhere in each of us. We all have times like that—times when an extra measure of care is needed. We need comfort and so does everyone else. And it's nothing to be ashamed of.

A friend dreamed of going to medical school when he was young. Growing up, he worked in his father's small auto-repair shop, but he knew that one day he was going to be a doctor. That dream never came true. When he was finishing high school, his father had a heart attack, and my friend took over the business to support the family.

"Sure I'd like to have been a doctor," he says, "but what's a person to do? It was tough to let go of that dream, but I've found a lot of satisfaction in my work, even though I didn't think life would work out this way."

All through our lives there are resignations of wishes. As children, once we learn to walk, we must resign ourselves to not being a baby anymore. If we just want to be taken care of and not make any effort to do more and more for ourselves, then we can avoid that resignation and just stay a baby.

You may know some adults who are still babies. Even though they're mentally and physically able people, they still want to be served all the time. How sad for them, not to have been able to experience the excitement of growing from one part of life to another.

One evening, as I sat at the piano, I began to play a song—almost without thinking. Little by little, the words came to me, and I realized it was a song I had known for many years about all our wishes coming true. It was called, "When You Wish Upon a Star." I remember when I was a boy and first heard that song, I had such a wonderful feeling. To think that wishing could make things come true was such a splendid idea to me. And I had lots of wishes.

But, years later, playing that song and

thinking those words, it dawned on me how important it was that all my wishes had *not* come true; of course, it was equally important that some of them actually had. And I wondered about the difference.

"When you wish upon a star . . ." Why, there are whole galaxies that we haven't even discovered yet, stars way out in space and stars within ourselves that are patiently waiting to be hitched to the work of our lives to brighten up our world.

I don't know your wishes or your hopes. Nobody but you and the people you care to share them with should know them. Wishes are sometimes grand and far beyond the reality of the present, but other wishes

are intimate. They are about simple
things . . . simple private things.

I trust that you'll feel good enough about
yourself to do all you can to help the best of
your wishes come true.

There would be no art, and there would be no science, if human beings had no desire to create. And if we had everything we ever needed or wanted, we would have no reason for creating anything. So, at the root of all art and all science there exists a gap—a gap between what the world is like and what we wish and hope for it to be like. Our unique way of bridging that gap in each of our lives seems to me to be the essence of the reason for human creativity.

Try your best to make goodness attractive.
That's one of the toughest assignments
you'll ever be given.

The most important moments are rarely in the bright lights with cameras rolling and mikes recording. The most important moments are rarely center stage; they most often happen "in the wings."

Have you found that to be true, too? That what you expected to be the big occasion or the main event turned out to be merely an excuse for you to be somewhere in order to be touched by something you might have otherwise considered of little importance?

It is tempting to cling to the familiar. Just like in music, if we keep living . . . playing in the key of C, we wouldn't have to take any risks of not making it to the key of E-flat. But we'd never know what it sounded like unless we tried. And once we've had the practice and the pleasure of making a transition from one key to the next, the subsequent times might not be quite so difficult.

We don't always succeed in what we try—certainly not by the world's standards—but I think you'll find it's the willingness to keep trying that matters most.

You can't be a winner all the time.

No matter what our age, no matter what our condition, life's disappointments often show us the limits of what we're able to do. But, of course, in dealing with them, we just might create a new forward striving.

When we're taking risks at any time in our lives, trying new things, whether it's a new job, or a diet, or a different lifestyle, it certainly helps to know that people who love us will urge us to keep trying, and will also offer a hand, an ear, or even a shoulder to cry on when we feel like giving up. Maybe, too, they'll help us remember, even as we're disappointed about what we can't do, that there is much we *can* do.

"You shall know the truth, and the truth
shall make you free."

It's hard for me to believe that it was 1946
when I last sat in this room looking up at
those words above this stage. I can tell you,
most of my thoughts during my
commencement week had to do with plans
for the summer or the next year, certainly
not fifty years from then! In fact, if somebody
had told me that I would go to college and
study music and theology and finally
produce television programs for young
children, I wouldn't have believed them.

For one thing, I thought I was going to be

an airline pilot. (I took flying lessons all during my senior year at the Latrobe Airport.) Obviously I didn't make that dream come true. It was as if I was meant to do something I never even thought about. How could I have thought about it? In those days, hardly anybody was thinking about television!

Yet all the while, somewhere inside of me, I carried those words, "The truth shall make you free." And I tried almost unconsciously to discover the truth about who I was and about my neighbor (the person I happened to be with at the moment). I found out, at every turn in the road, that truth seemed to set me free enough to go on.

Dr. Fred Rainsberry was the person who first put me in front of the television camera. For eight years I had co-produced a daily program called *The Children's Corner.* I wrote and played the music and voiced the puppets all behind the set.

When Dr. Rainsberry, the head of children's programming, asked me to work for his department at the Canadian Broadcasting Corporation, he said, "Fred, I've seen you talk with kids. Let's put you yourself on the air." I told him I'd never done such a thing, but he replied, "Let's give it a try. We'll call it 'Misterogers.'" His confidence and support launched me into something I may have never dared to do on my own.

Fifty years from now I trust that you'll look back over your journey and recognize the blessings—great and small—which helped to carry you through, and also realize how other people shared their truth and their light with you and made the trip less lonely.

You know, none of us gets to be competent, mature people without the help of others. By now you've discovered that you don't have to go it alone. In fact, no one gets to be a graduate without the investment of other people: people who have loved you all along the way.

During this extra-special time, I'd like to give you a minute to think of those who have believed in you . . . those who have helped you live your life knowing what was good and real. A minute of silence for all of us to remember those who have cared about us through our lives: people who have made a significant difference in our being who we are right now. One minute of silence.

Whomever you've been thinking about, whether they're here or far away or even in heaven, imagine how pleased they'd be to know that you recognize what a difference they've made in your becoming. And I trust that you'll discover how much our world needs your truth.

I'm Proud of You

I'm proud of you. I'm proud of you.
I hope that you're as proud as I am.

And that you're
Learning how important you are,
How important each person you see can be.
Discovering each one's specialty
Is the most important learning.

I'm proud of you. I'm proud of you.
I hope that you are proud of you, too!

I'm proud of you for the times you've said, "No," when all it seemed to mean was a loss of pleasure, yet eventually supported the growth of somebody else and yourself.

I'm proud of you for standing up for something you believed in—something that wasn't particularly popular, but that assured the rights of someone less fortunate than you.

I'm proud of you for times you wrestled with your problems and discovered how much that helped you to grow.

I'm proud of you for anything that allows you to feel proud of yourself.

You will be the senators and the doctors and the nurses and the lawyers and the educators and the mothers and the fathers of the next generation, and I trust that you'll have the opportunity to participate fully in this wonderful world of ours. You'll be the ones who will make the decisions. You'll be the ones who will make the difference. I trust as time goes on, you will be aware deep inside yourself of the kind of difference you have been privileged to make.

May you seek out your own continuing life education and, over time, over your whole lifetime, may you grow in faith and reverence, uprightness in morals, knowledge of language and arts, forgiveness, honesty, commitment, maturity, and your capacity to love.

You'll be the one to decide your next steps . . . and the next steps won't all be easy—not by any means—but if they're honest, they'll be worth the try. Any real work has its tough times (you know that), and any real love has its trials. I wish you the kind of life's work in which you can use the greatest part of who you are; and I wish you the kind of life's love that will enhance all that you do, as well as all that you are.

My hope for you at the beginning of this new moment in your life is that you will take good care of that part of you where your best dreams come from, that invisible part of you that allows you to look on yourself and your neighbor with delight. Do your best to appreciate the gifts that you really are and always will be . . . to look for every opportunity that allows you to clap and cheer, loving your neighbor as yourself.

ACKNOWLEDGMENTS

Here at Family Communications, Inc. (FCI), we feel privileged to have shared so much of Fred Rogers' journey. Many of us on the staff have had the pleasure and benefit of years and years of working closely with him. His philosophy became a part of our understanding of children, the media, and ourselves.

Even now, Fred Rogers' vision lights the way for our journey. His beacon shines on the good work of our past that's endured over the years. He strengthened and enabled us, individually and collectively as a company. So we continue to offer and build on *Mister Rogers' Neighborhood* and the related materials that we developed under his leadership. At the same time, Fred's pioneering spirit calls on us to forge ahead and blaze new trails, much as he did in his lifetime. As new media and new concerns in today's world emerge, we're heading into new territory, always guided by his mission of supporting what's healthy in human beings, young and old.

But Fred Rogers wasn't part of just our professional lives. He was part of our personal journeys. He genuinely cared about us and our families, comforting us in our tough times, supporting us when we felt challenged, and celebrating our joys and proud moments right along with us. What he gave to the world—through *Mister Rogers' Neighborhood*, his speeches, and his writings—he gave to us in a very real and personal way. We knew we had an invitation to share with him the stories of our lives, and he listened with all his heart. Our journeys became part of his. Now that he's "way beyond our sight," he's still very much a part of each of us.

These days, our journey at FCI has been greatly strengthened by our ongoing partnerships. A heartfelt thanks goes to our good friend Bob Miller, president of Hyperion, who, after the enormous success of *The World*

According to Mister Rogers, encouraged us to continue bringing more of Fred's timeless wisdom to share with our "neighbors." We were also fortunate that Bob gave us another opportunity to work with our editor, Mary Ellen O'Neill, who is such a great appreciator of Fred's work and his words.

We know that our partnerships, like this one with Hyperion, don't happen by magic or overnight. They happen in large measure because of our FCI president, Bill Isler, who has a remarkable ability to create connections—and solidify them. We're also deeply grateful for the unwavering support of the Rogers family, especially Joanne Rogers, who has taken on the chairmanship of the FCI board. Joanne's visits to our office always mean rounds of hugs and sounds of laughter. A huge thanks goes to two of our staff members, Hedda Bluestone Sharapan and Cathy Cohen Droz, who worked collaboratively, taking on the task of gathering, sifting through, and organizing the wealth of material for this book. Thanks, too, to everyone at FCI and on our board, who, directly or indirectly, have contributed to this body of work.

As we continue our journey here at FCI, we're all grateful to be entrusted with Fred Rogers' legacy, guided by his philosophy, strengthened by his dedication, and inspired by his vision.

BIOGRAPHY OF
FRED ROGERS

Fred McFeely Rogers was best known as "Mister Rogers," creator, host, writer, composer, and puppeteer for the longest-running program on PBS, *Mister Rogers' Neighborhood*.

His journey to the *Neighborhood* began in 1951 during his senior year at Rollins College, when he became intrigued by the educational potential of television. After graduating with a degree in music composition from Rollins, he joined NBC in New York as an assistant producer for *The Kate Smith Hour, The Voice of Firestone*, and the *NBC Opera Theatre*. In 1952, he married Joanne Byrd, a pianist and fellow Rollins graduate.

Returning to his hometown area of western Pennsylvania in 1953, he helped found Pittsburgh's public television station, WQED, and co-produced an hour-long live daily children's program, *The Children's Corner,* for which he also worked behind the scenes as puppeteer and musician. To broaden his understanding of children, Fred Rogers began his lifelong study of children and families at the Graduate School of Child Development in the University of Pittsburgh School of Medicine. There he had the opportunity to work closely with young children under the supervision of Dr. Margaret B. McFarland, clinical psychologist. He also completed a Master of Divinity degree at the Pittsburgh Theological Seminary and was ordained as a Presbyterian minister in 1963 with the unique charge of serving children and families through the media.

Fred Rogers has been the recipient of virtually every major award in television and education. He has received honorary degrees from more than forty colleges and universities, and in 2002 was awarded the Presidential Medal of Freedom, the nation's highest civilian honor.

In 1971, Fred Rogers founded Family Communications,

Inc. (FCI), a non-profit company for the production of *Mister Rogers' Neighborhood* and other materials. Building on its beginnings in broadcast television production, FCI has expanded into almost all forms of media—print, audio, video, training workshops, the Internet, DVD, and traveling exhibits. For information about Family Communications, visit the website (www.fci.org).

The company's ongoing work continues to be guided by Fred Rogers' mission of communicating with young children and their families in clear, honest, nurturing, and supportive ways.